Bacteria and viruses

Carol Bryan and Bobbie Neate

Bacteria and viruses have many similarities but they have many differences. Read chapter 1 about bacteria and chapter 9 about viruses. You can then compare the two organisms.

Contents

1	What are bacteria?	2
2	Why we have bacteria	4
3	How helpful bacteria work in our digestive system	6
4	How small are bacteria?	8
5	What shape are bacteria?	10
6	Where are harmful bacteria found?	12
7	How harmful bacteria invade our body	14
8	Fighting harmful bacteria – the immune system	16
9	What are viruses?	18
10	What do viruses do?	20
11	How do viruses work? How do they invade our body?	22
12	How small are viruses?	24
13	What shape are viruses?	26
14	Keeping healthy	28
	Glossary	30
	Further information	31
	Index	32

1 What are bacteria?

Bacteria are very small living things. Bacteria can be helpful or harmful.

The word '**bacterium**' comes from a Greek word meaning 'rod'. The plural of bacterium is bacteria.

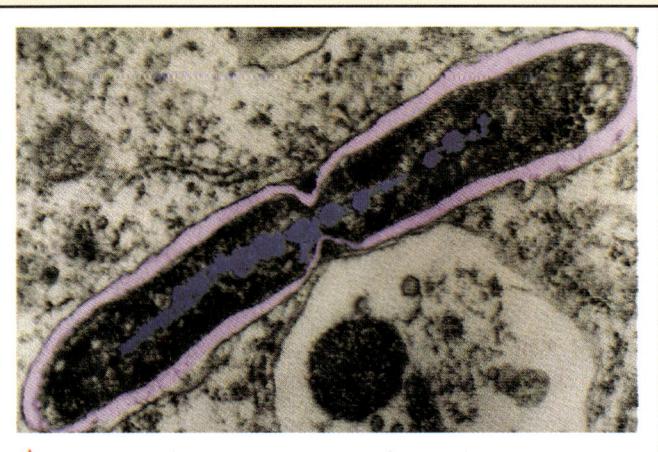

⬆ A magnified photograph of a bacterium.

⬆ Sneezing can spread bacteria into the air.

Bacteria are one of many different kinds of organism in the world. All living creatures are organisms. We are organisms and so are bacteria. Bacteria are so small that they can only be seen through a microscope.

Helpful bacteria live in our large bowel, which is part of our digestive system. These bacteria make our digestive system work better. They can be found in the digestive systems of all mammals. Helpful bacteria also live in our throats and noses and on our skin. Harmful bacteria invade our bodies when we do not want them to. They make us unwell and, sometimes, very seriously ill. These bacteria can be found in the air, in food, in soil and in water.

Bacteria can be in water.

Bacteria can be in the soil.

2 Why we have bacteria

Helpful bacteria make our bodies work better. Without them we can become very ill.

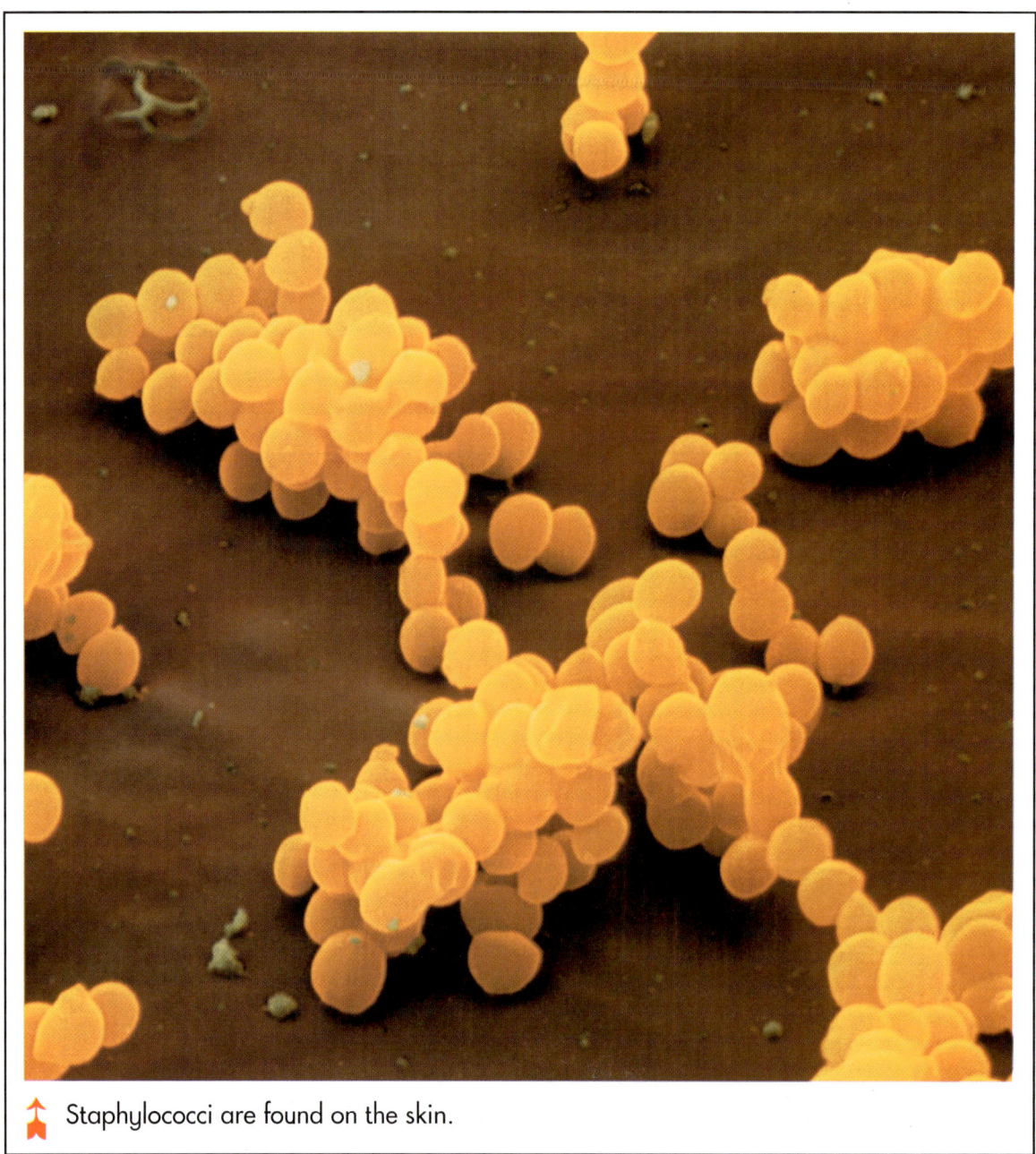

↑ Staphylococci are found on the skin.

Bacteria help us keep healthy in different ways. We find them in our digestive system, in our noses and throats and on our skin.

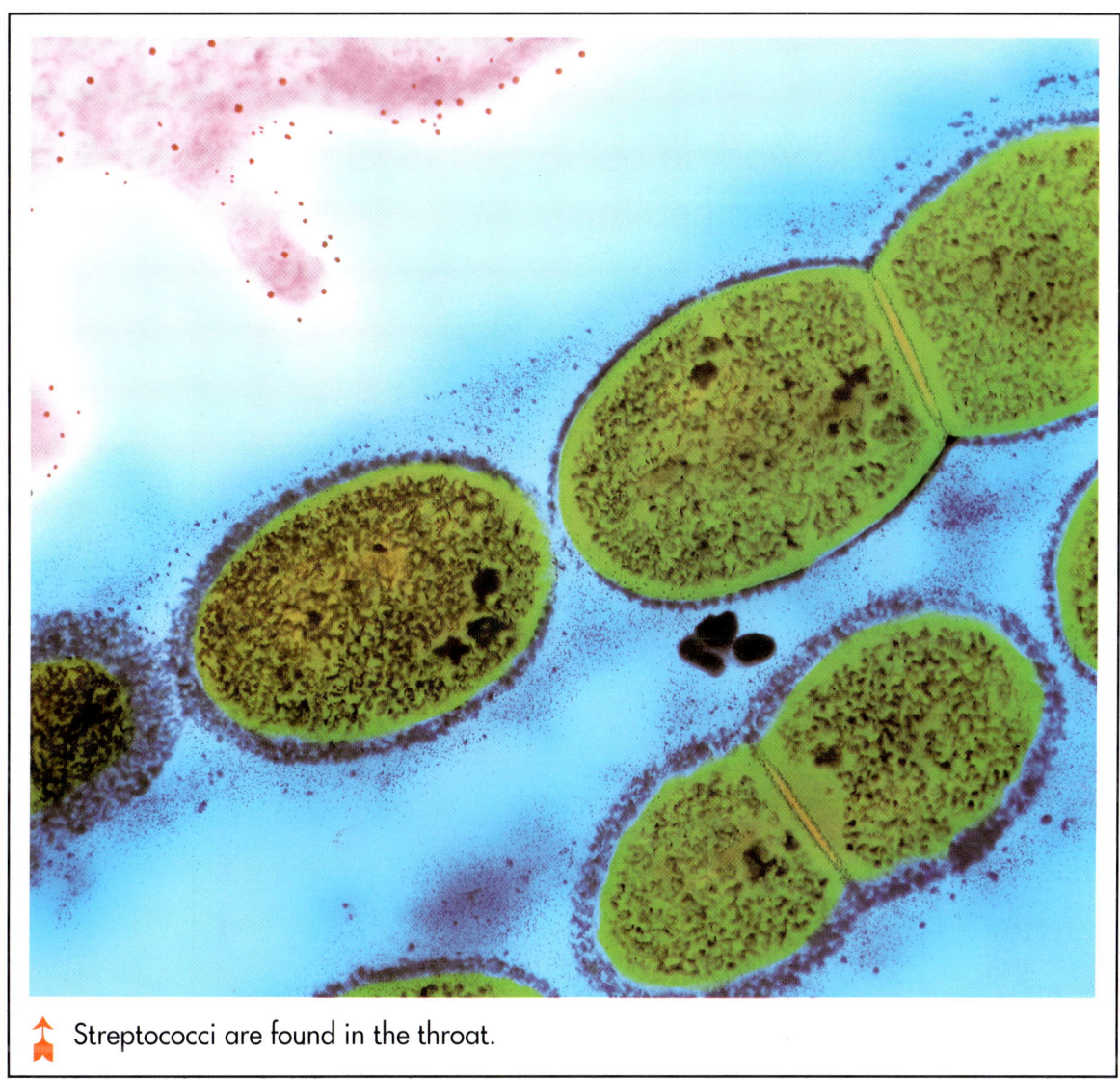

Streptococci are found in the throat.

Bacteria in our digestive system make vitamins which are useful to the body. These bacteria also break down parts of food which are not needed by the body.

Bacteria on our skin can produce special substances which help to protect us against harmful bacteria. Staphylococcus is one of these.

There are colonies of bacteria in our throats and noses which can help to keep us healthy. Streptococcus is one of these bacteria.

3 How helpful bacteria work in our digestive system

Helpful bacteria work in our large bowel. They help us to keep healthy.

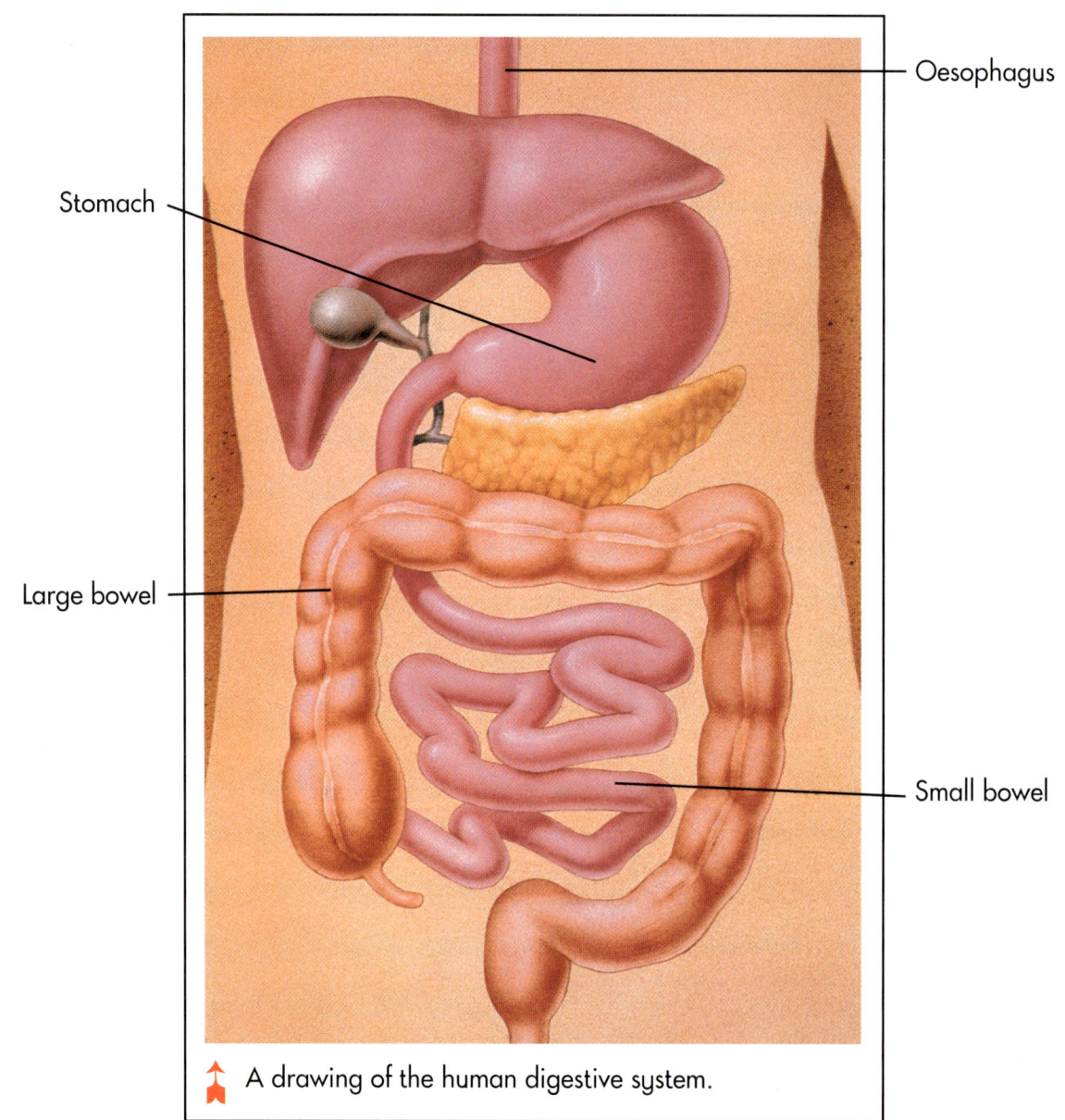

↑ A drawing of the human digestive system.

Our digestive system consists of the mouth, the oesophagus, the stomach, the small bowel and the large bowel. Food passes through each part until the waste products are formed into stools, which are then passed when we go to the lavatory.

We have a digestive system which breaks down the food we eat. This system takes all the useful parts from the food we eat and gives it to our blood. The blood then carries these around the body to wherever they are needed.

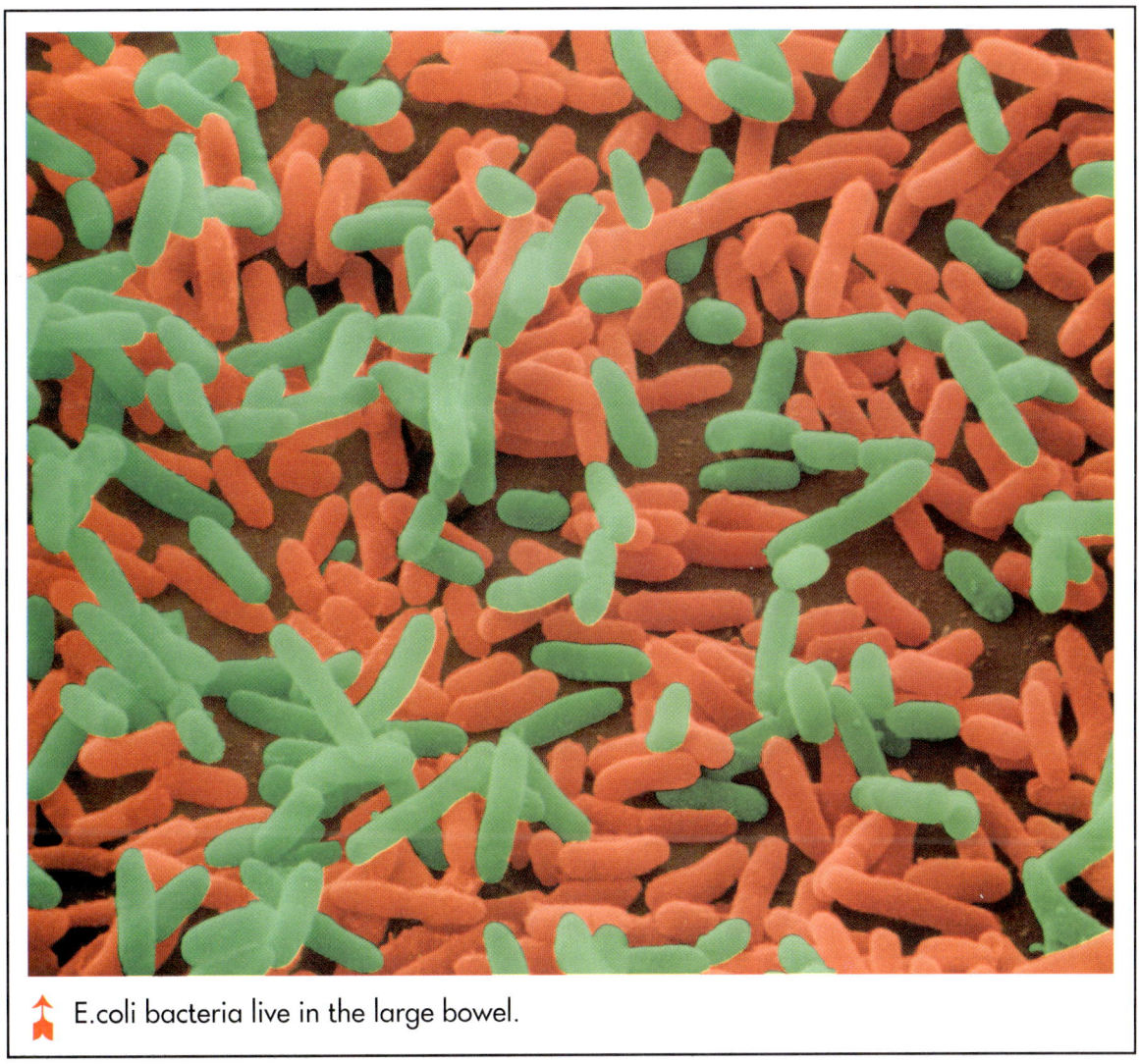

⬆ E.coli bacteria live in the large bowel.

However, some parts of our food cannot be used by our bodies. These waste products of the things we eat are made into stools in the large bowel. Bacteria are busy working in our large bowel to help these processes happen.

4 How small are bacteria?

Bacteria are very, very tiny. You cannot see them without a microscope.

← Streptococci.

Bacteria can only be seen through a microscope.
They are so small that you could fit over a thousand
of the smaller bacteria on one pin head.

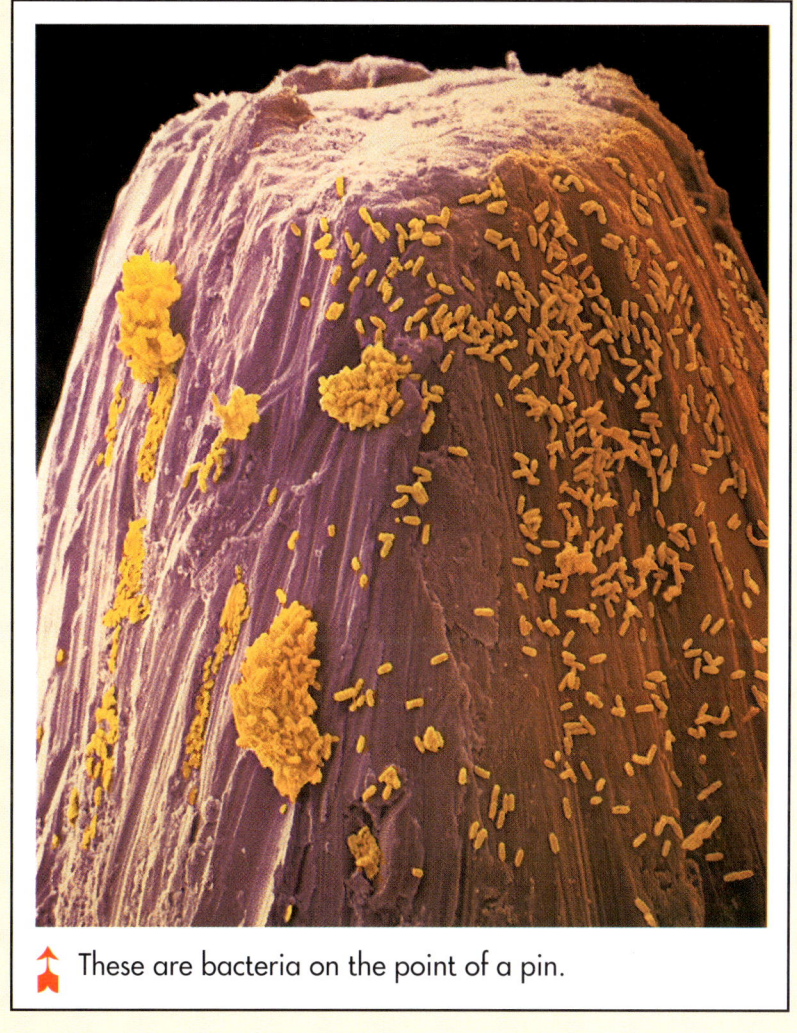

⬆ These are bacteria on the point of a pin.

Even though they are very small, bacteria do vary in size.
Some are ten times bigger than others. Bacteria tend to
live together in colonies. Often, over a thousand live in
the same colony.

5 What shape are bacteria?

Bacteria are not all the same shape. We put bacteria into groups because of their shape. This is called classification.

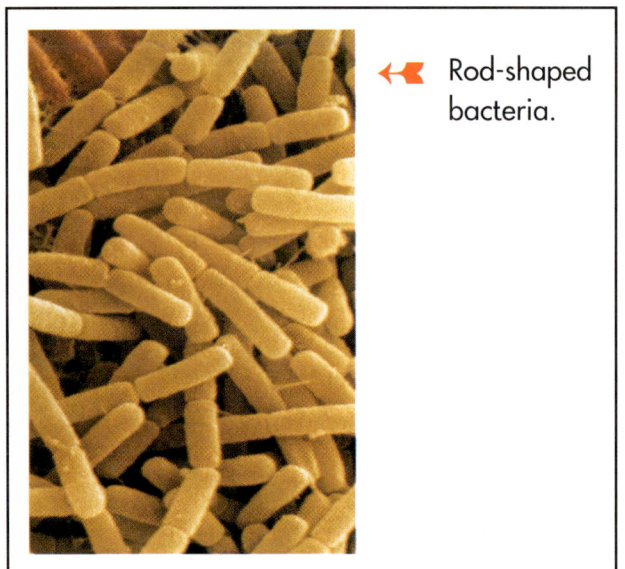

Rod-shaped bacteria.

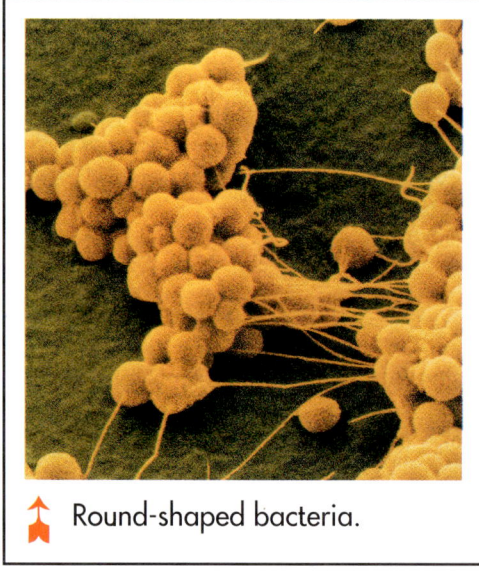

Round-shaped bacteria.

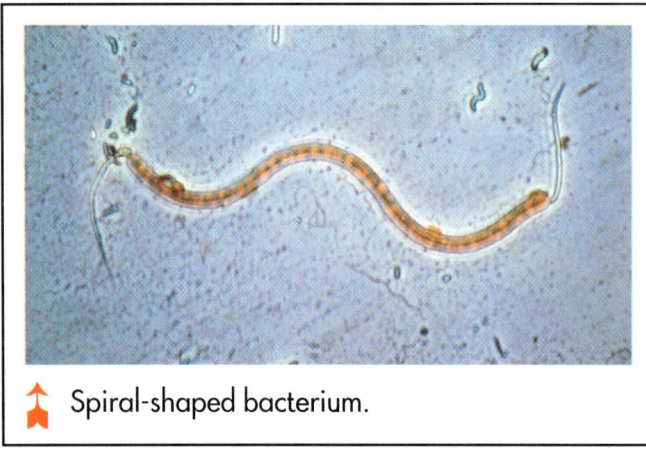

Spiral-shaped bacterium.

Bacteria can be round, rod-shaped or spiral.

Streptococci are round bacteria. They can cause a sore throat.

Salmonella are rod-shaped bacteria. They can cause very bad food poisoning.

Leptospira is a spiral bacterium. It can cause meningitis.

E.coli are rod-shaped bacteria. They are found in our large bowel and are very helpful. However, when these bacteria leave our bowel they can cause diseases in other parts of our body such as the urinary tract (where urine is formed).

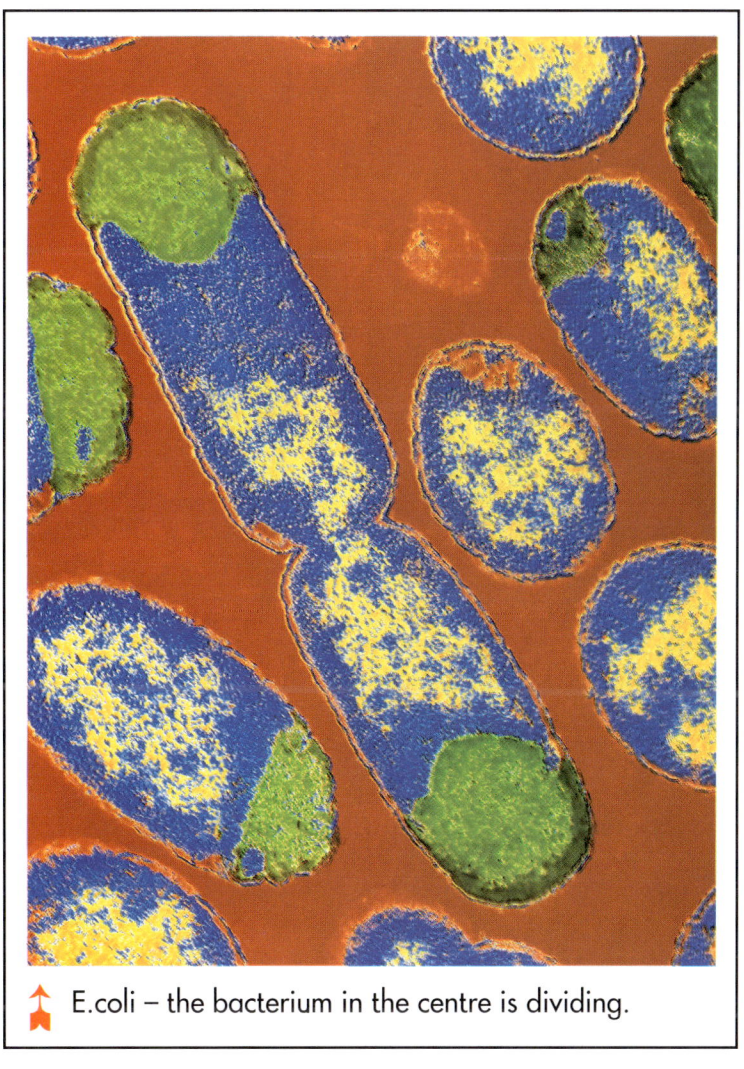

⬆ E.coli – the bacterium in the centre is dividing.

6 Where are harmful bacteria found?

Harmful bacteria are all around us. They are found in food, in water, in soil and in the air.

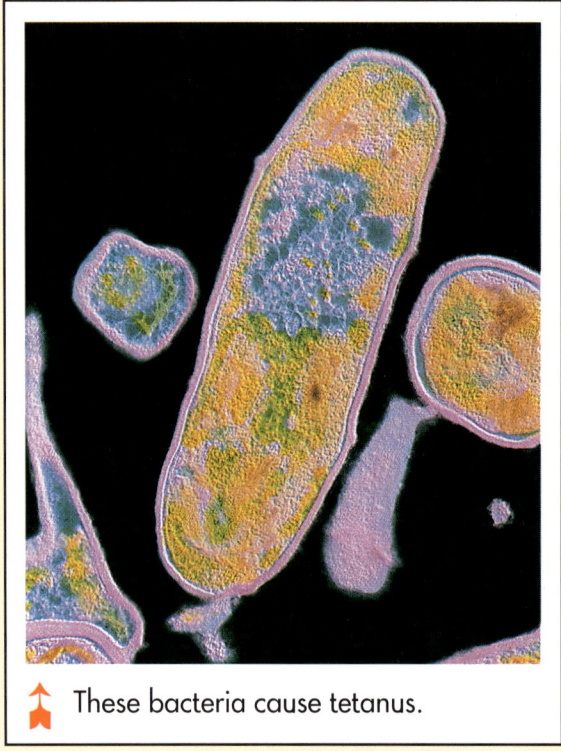

⬆ These bacteria cause tetanus.

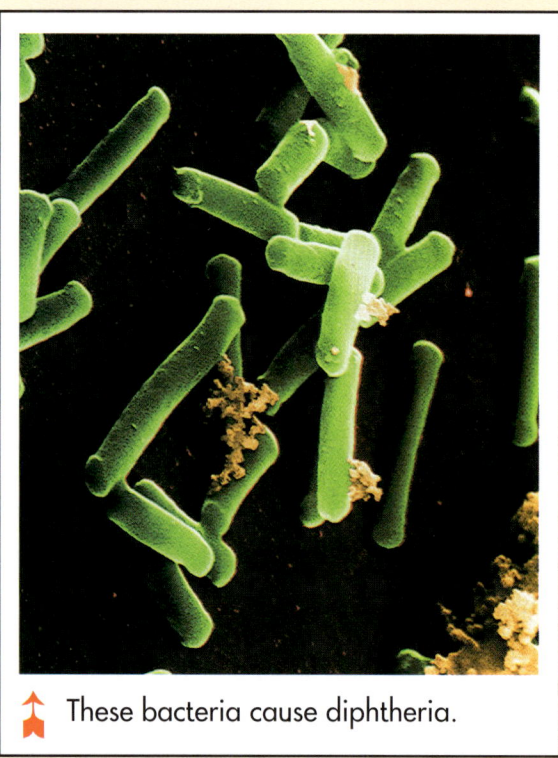

⬆ These bacteria cause diphtheria.

Bacteria are everywhere. They can survive in the most unpleasant conditions. Most of them can survive very hot, very cold, very dry and very wet conditions.

But some weaker bacteria can be killed very easily.

Salmonella is found in food. It causes diarrhoea.

The bacteria which cause the diseases typhoid and dysentery are found in water.

Corynebacterium diphtheriae is found in the air and causes a very serious throat infection called diphtheria.

Clostridium Tetani is found in the soil and causes the muscles to stiffen. This is known as tetanus.

All of these bacteria can be killers.

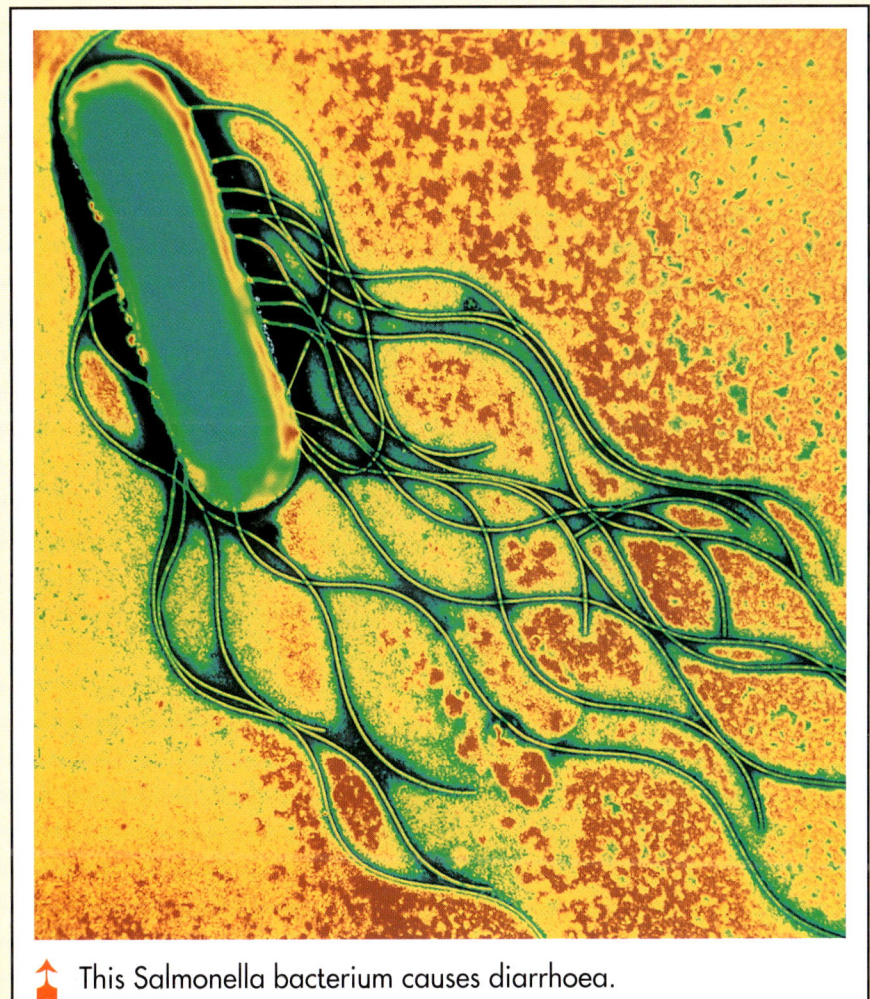

⬆ This Salmonella bacterium causes diarrhoea.

7 How harmful bacteria invade our body

Bacteria invade our bodies very easily. We can breathe them or swallow them in our food or water. They can invade cuts in our skin.

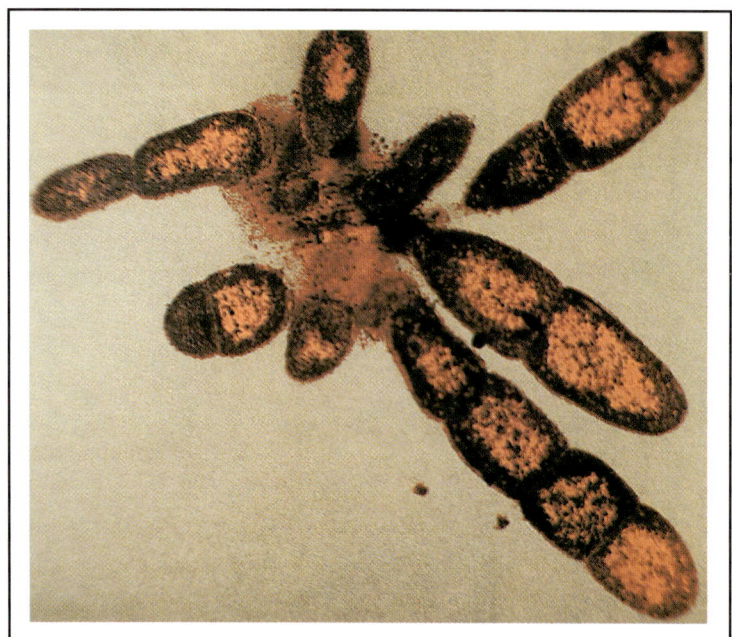

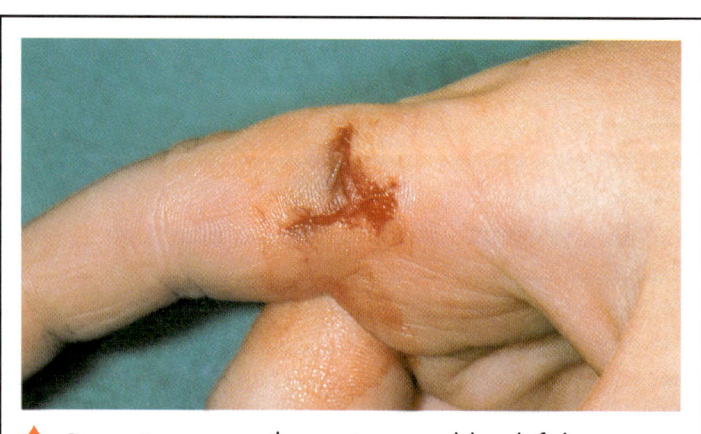

⬆ Bacteria can easily get into our blood if the skin is cut.

When our skin is cut, bacteria invade our blood. We also swallow bacteria and these can cause trouble with our digestive systems. The bacteria we breathe can cause problems with our lungs and our throats. All these bacteria make toxins. Toxins are harmful to the body.

Bacteria invade every person's body whether they are healthy or not. Bacteria do not need to enter our body cells to cause damage. Viruses do. Bacteria do not need to enter our bodies to multiply. Viruses do.

Bacteria are able to do more damage to the very old or the very young. With older people, this is because their immune system does not work so effectively anymore. With babies, their immune system is not fully developed so it has not yet started to work effectively.

People who are not very healthy may become more unwell from harmful bacteria than healthy people.

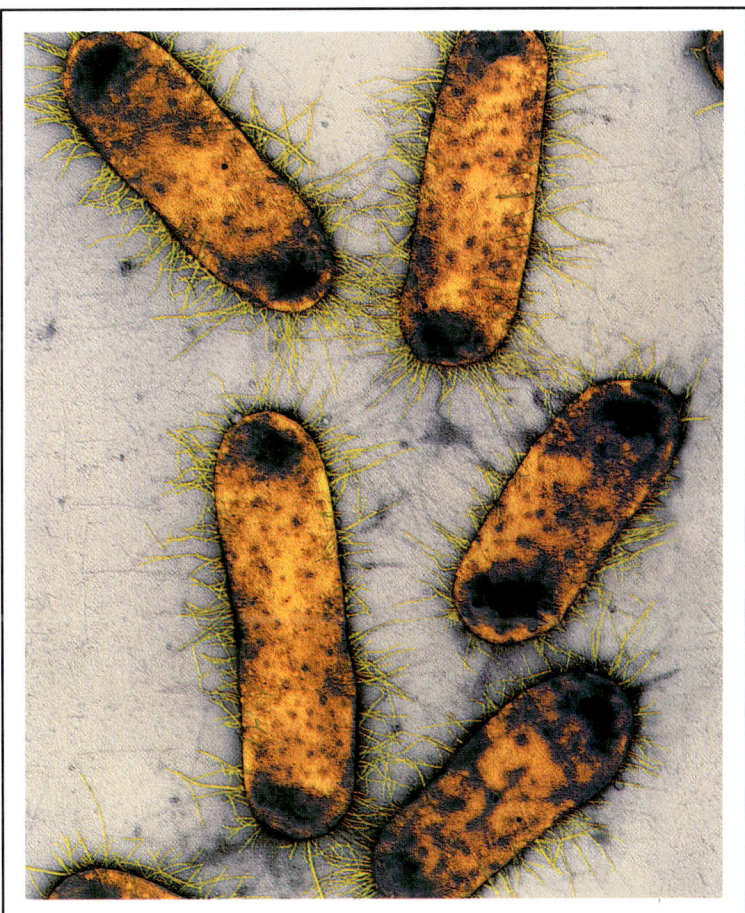

A bacterium has pili which look like hairs. These pili can attach to other bacterium.

8 Fighting harmful bacteria – the immune system

All humans and mammals have an immune system. Our immune system helps defend us against bacteria and viruses.

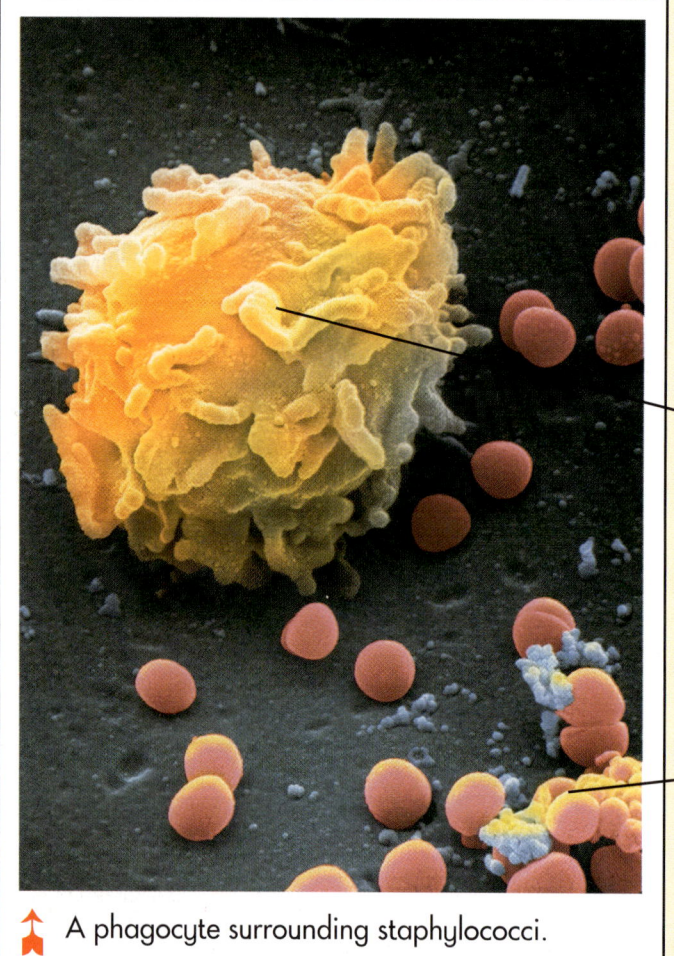

A phagocyte surrounding staphylococci.

In our bodies we have several systems which help us fight bacteria. One of these is a group of white blood cells which live in our blood. These white blood cells are able to capture and destroy bacteria. They are called phagocytes.

The body works effectively because it is able to know which organisms are invaders from outside. For example, when we have a cut in our skin, harmful bacteria get into our blood. These harmful bacteria are surrounded by phagocytes. These phagocytes wrap themselves around the harmful invaders and then gobble them up. The bacteria can no longer do us any harm. These phagocytes work very effectively.

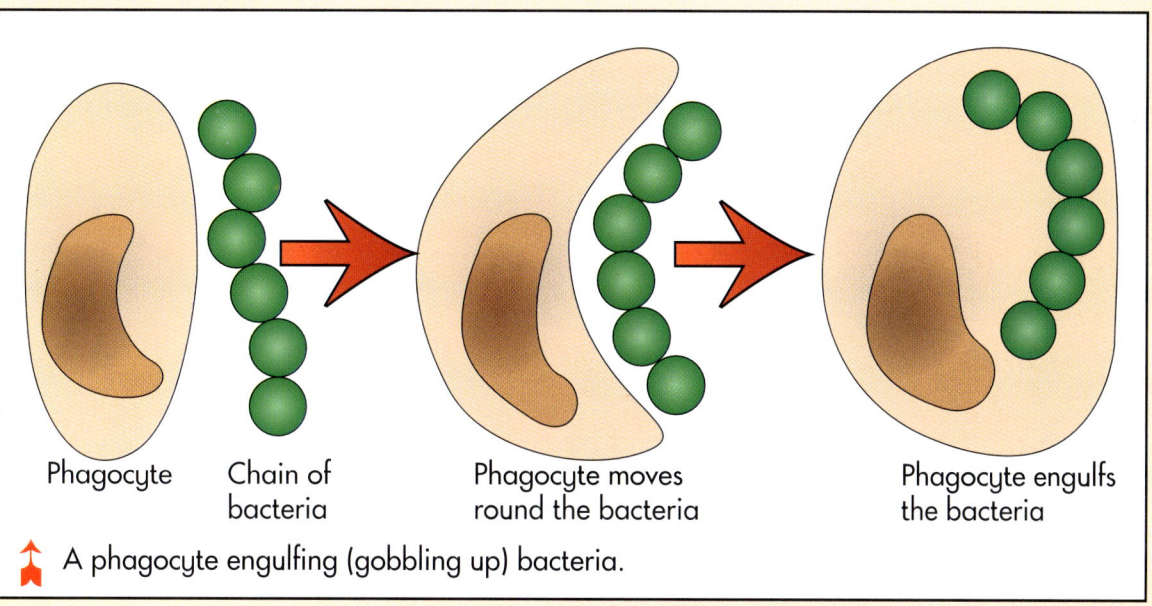

Phagocyte   Chain of bacteria   Phagocyte moves round the bacteria   Phagocyte engulfs the bacteria

A phagocyte engulfing (gobbling up) bacteria.

Antibiotics

When bacteria make us ill, we often need antibiotics.

Antibiotics are drugs which destroy bacteria.

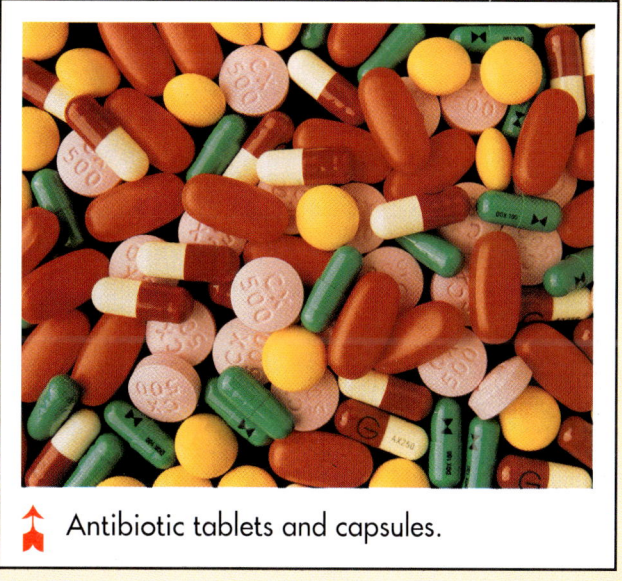

Antibiotic tablets and capsules.

9 What are viruses?

Viruses are very, very small living things. All viruses are harmful to humans and animals. There are no friendly viruses.

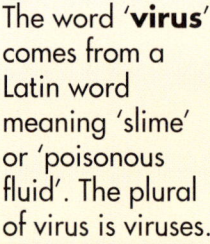

The word '**virus**' comes from a Latin word meaning 'slime' or 'poisonous fluid'. The plural of virus is viruses.

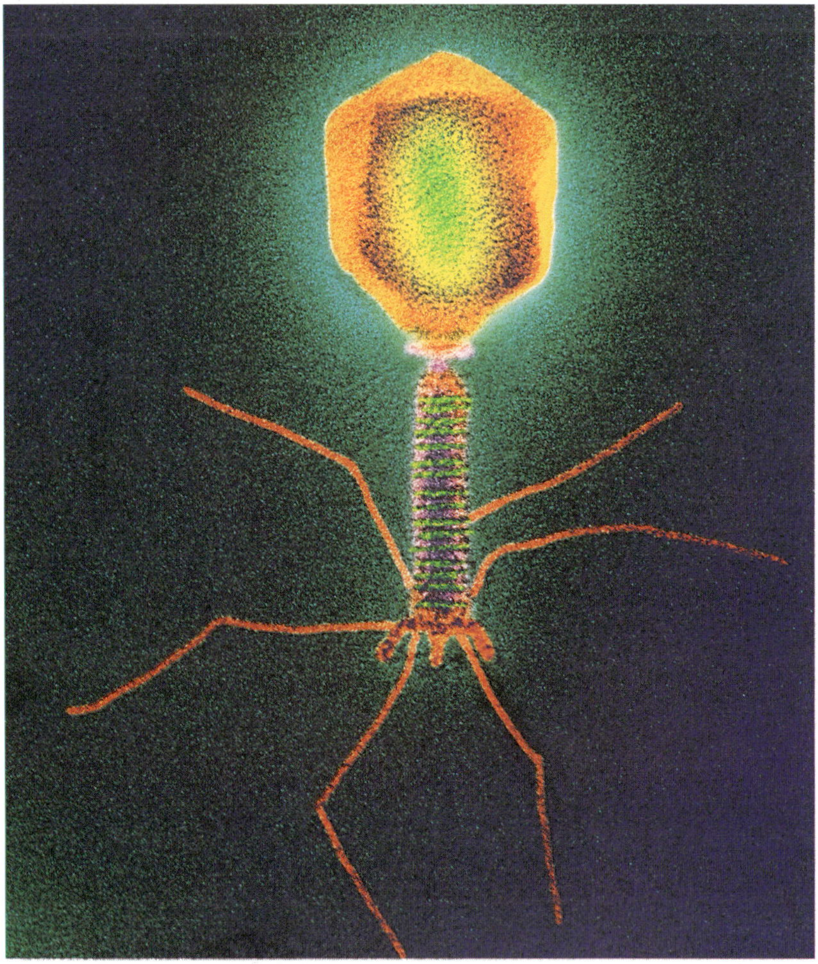

▲ A magnified photograph of a virus.

Viruses are one of the many different organisms in the world. Viruses are much smaller than bacteria. Viruses enter our bodies in lots of different ways. It is believed that all viruses are harmful.

Viruses are even smaller than bacteria. Experts think that all viruses are harmful and can sometimes make us very ill. Viruses must enter our body cells to reproduce themselves. Colds, influenza ('flu) and some sore throats are all caused by viruses. Viruses can enter our bodies very easily and in lots of different ways. We can breathe them in and they can get in through cuts. We can get viruses from contact with other people and with infected animals.

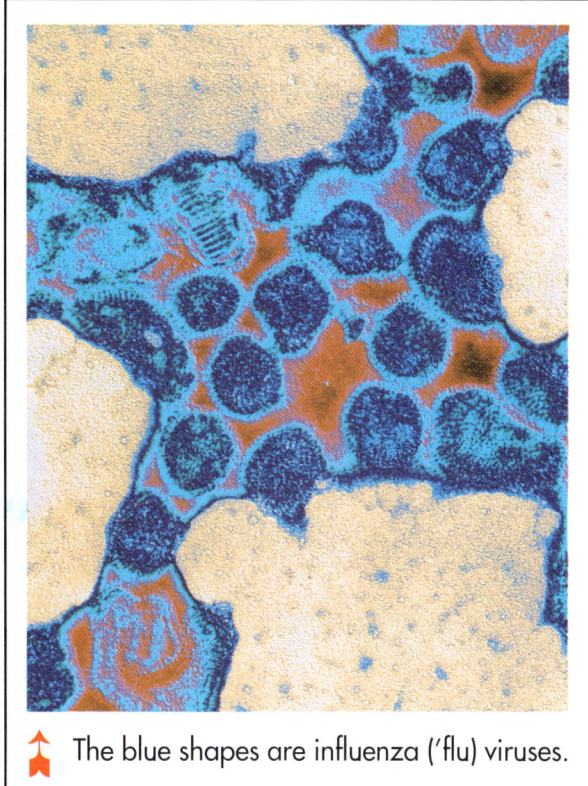

⬆ The blue shapes are influenza ('flu) viruses.

➡ The pink shapes are new HIV viruses being formed.

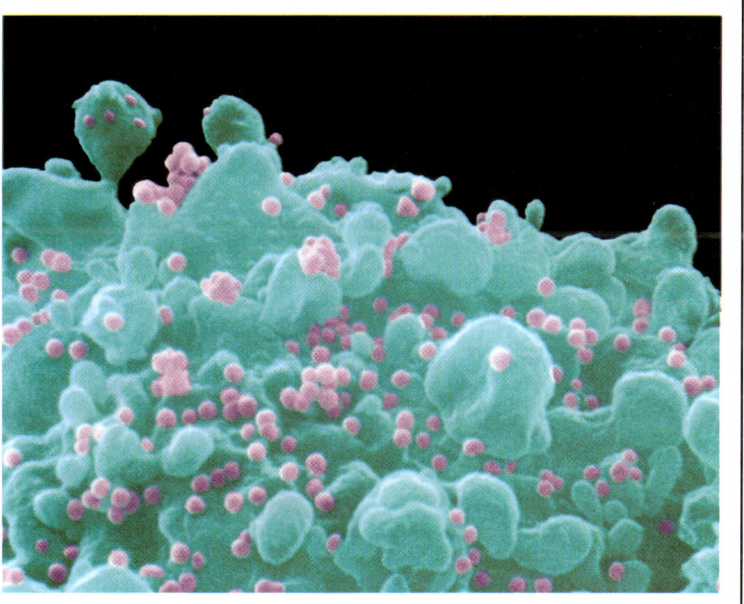

10 What do viruses do?

Most viruses do harm to humans and animals.

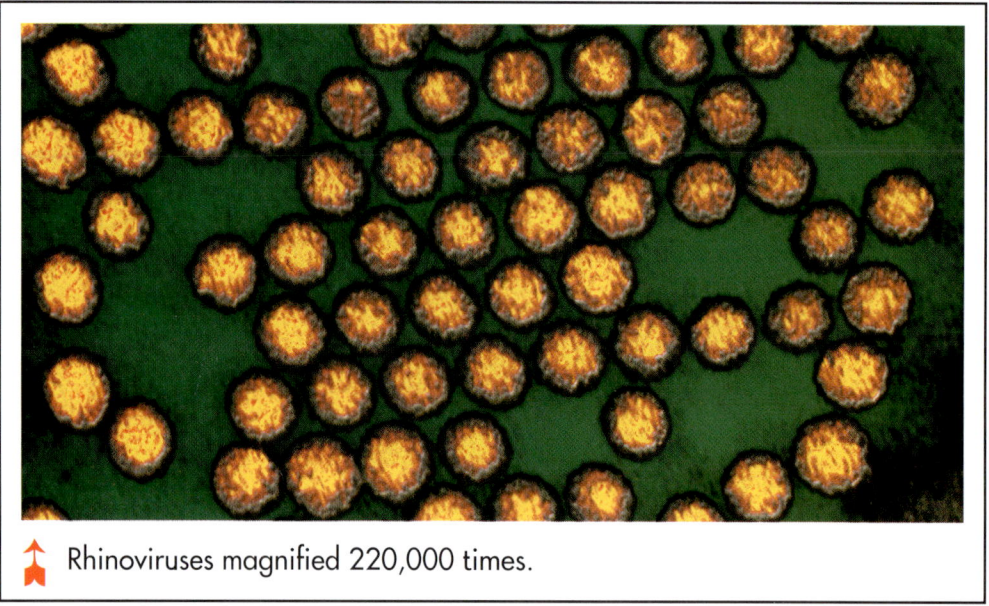

↑ Rhinoviruses magnified 220,000 times.

Viruses can make us ill. A virus called the Rhinovirus gives us colds. Another virus called the Adenovirus gives us sore throats.

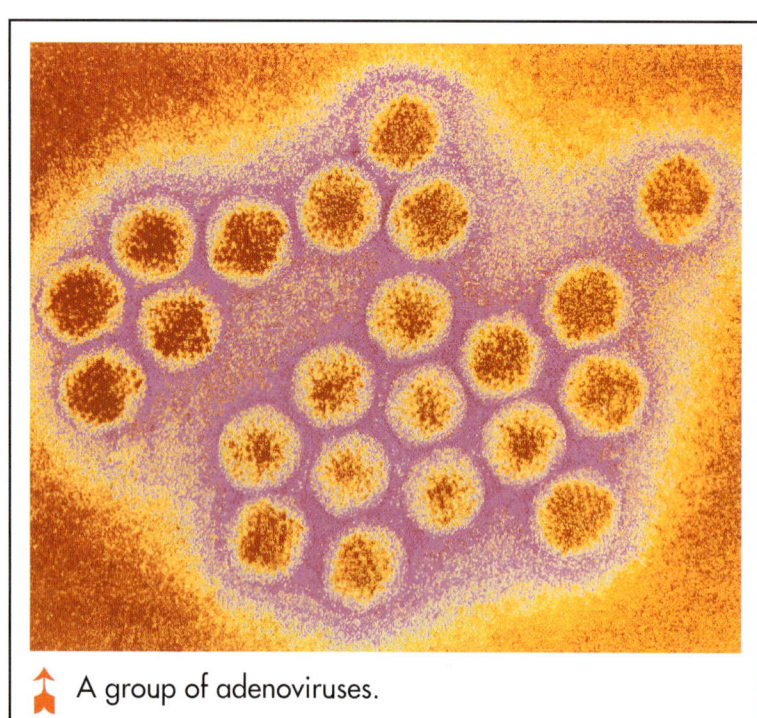

↑ A group of adenoviruses.

Different viruses have different effects. Most viruses will make us feel unwell for a while and then we get better. There are a few viruses that can make us very ill for a long time.

There are several ways our bodies can fight viruses. For instance, our body cells can produce substances called interferons which can prevent the virus attacking our cells.

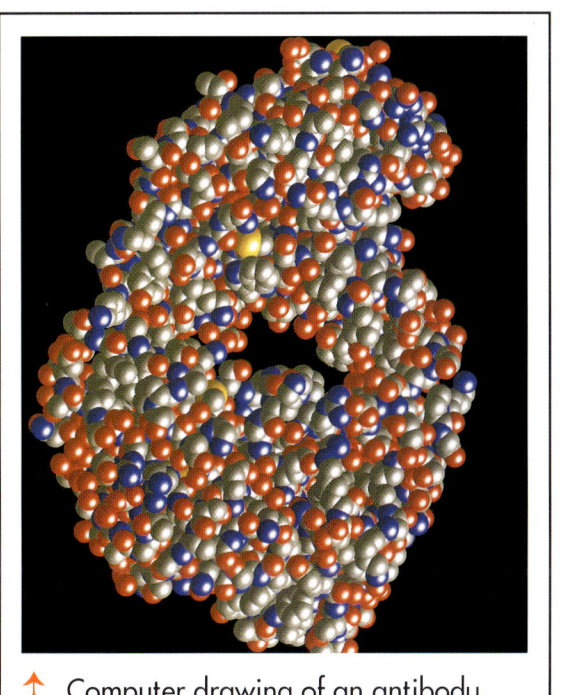

Computer drawing of an antibody.

Another system for fighting viruses is provided by our special blood cells called lymphocytes which produce antibodies when a virus invades the body. If a virus of the same type invades the body again, the antibodies are ready to attack the virus.

Immunisation helps the body produce antibodies. Injections against diseases such as whooping cough work in this way.

Vaccinations help us fight diseases.

11 How do viruses work?
How do they invade our body?

Viruses invade our bodies very easily. When viruses get into our bodies they are able to multiply.

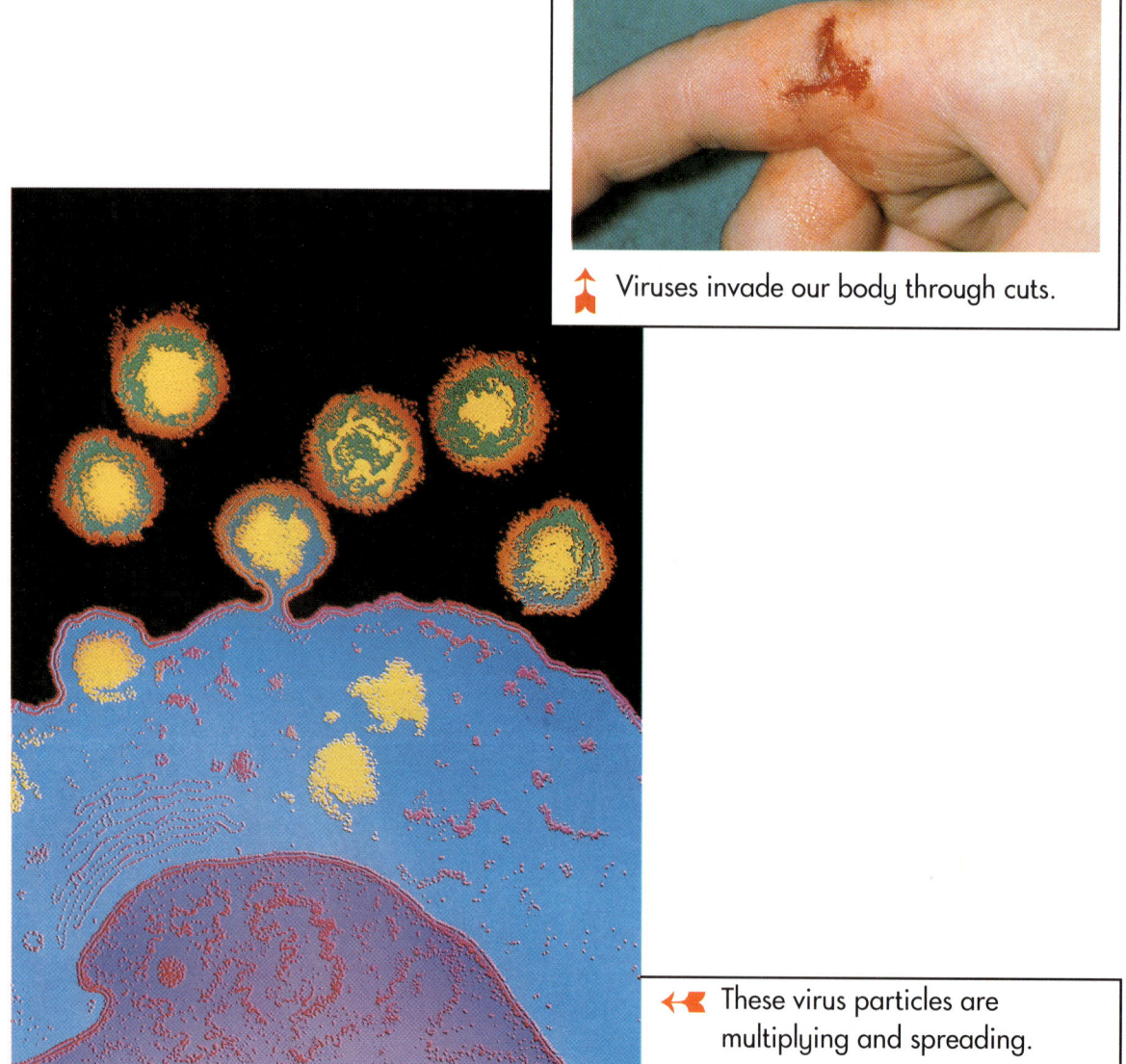

⬆ Viruses invade our body through cuts.

⬅ These virus particles are multiplying and spreading.

Viruses must have a host to multiply. A host is a plant or animal which allows a parasite to live on it. Any organism can be a host for a virus.

Viruses cannot work until they get into our body cells. Some cells are harmed by viruses straight away but some are harmed much later. When viruses get into our body cells, they are able to multiply and survive and there they will do damage. They use the special substances such as DNA or RNA which are inside our body cells to multiply. The virus is then able to make many new, small viruses which are called particles. These new viruses (particles) leave the cell and go off to find other cells to invade.

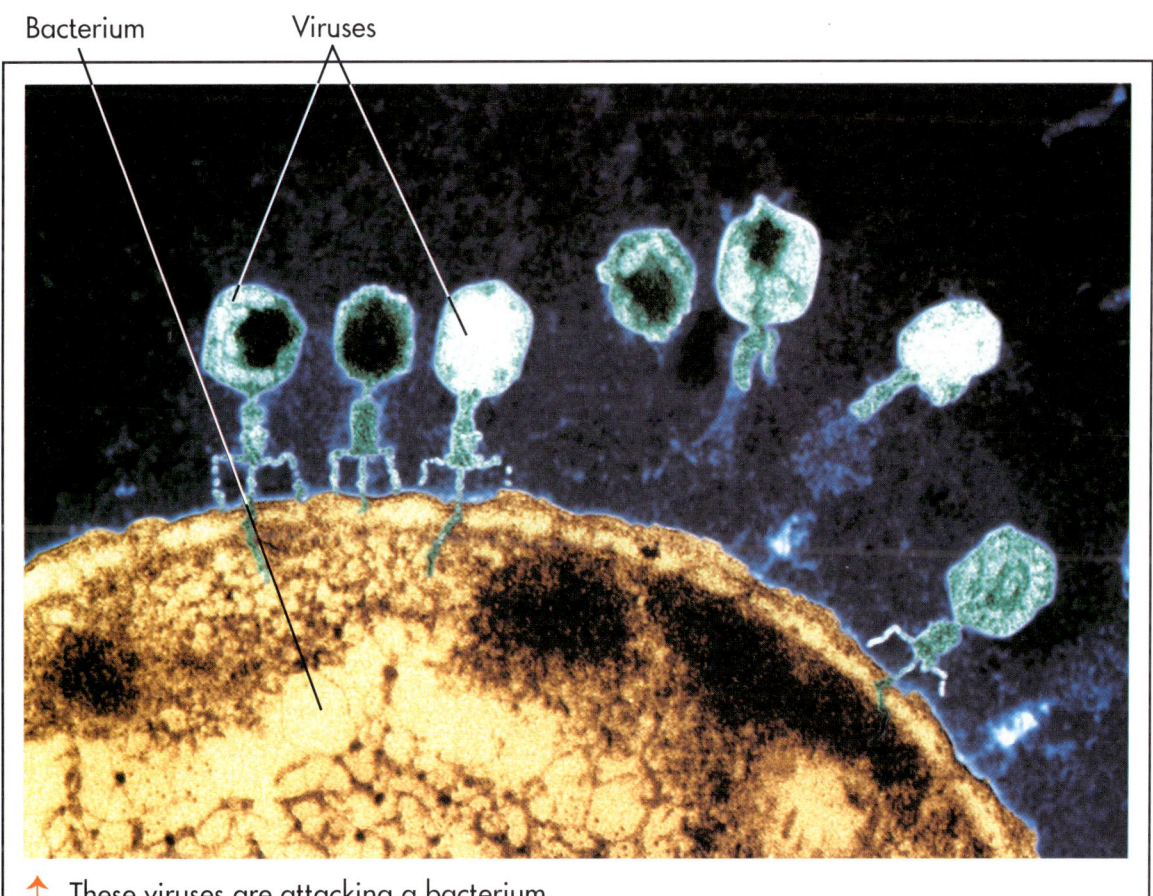

These viruses are attacking a bacterium.

12 How small are viruses?

Viruses are very, very small. You cannot see them without a very powerful microscope.

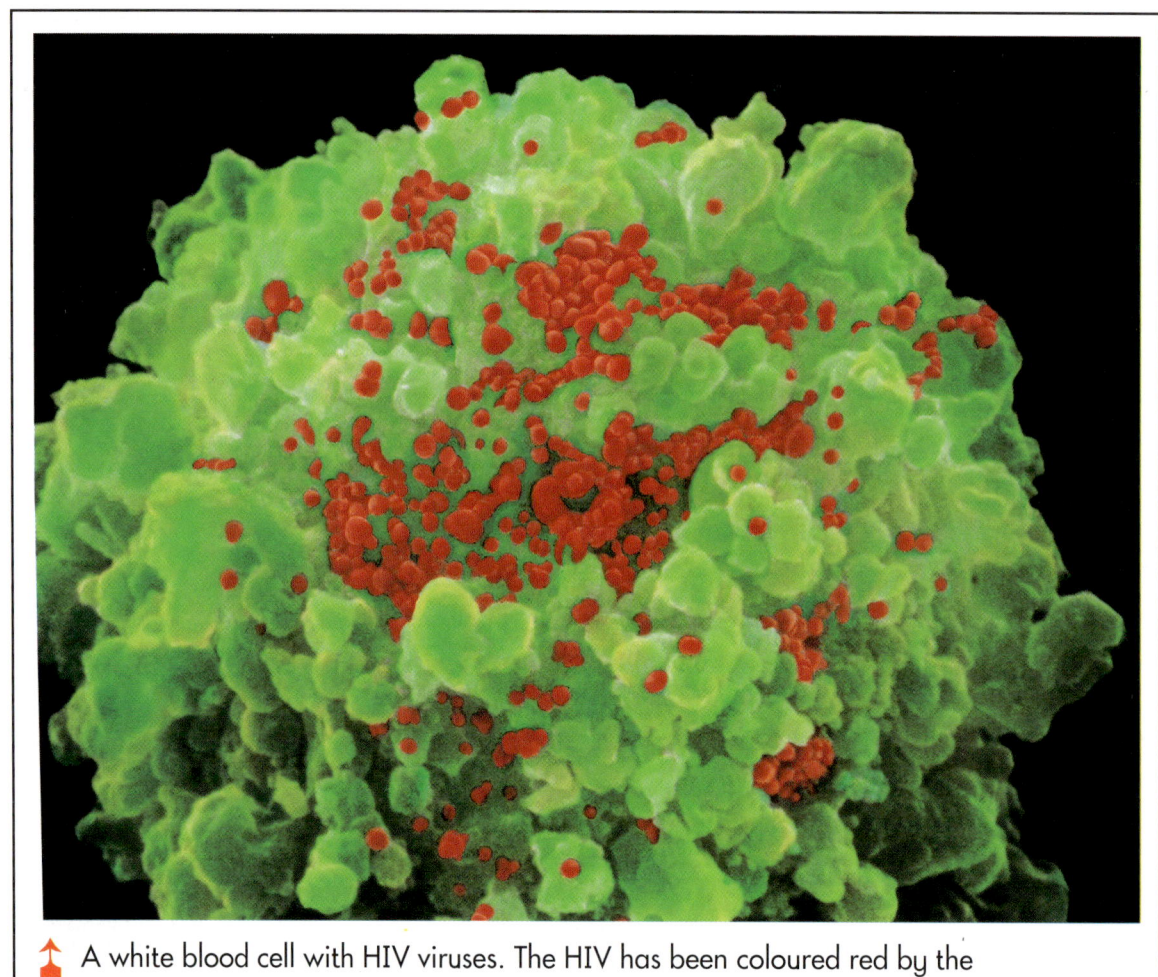

⬆ A white blood cell with HIV viruses. The HIV has been coloured red by the photographer. This virus is very small.

Viruses can only be seen through a very powerful microscope called an electron microscope. Viruses can be a hundred times smaller than bacteria.

Even though viruses are so small, they do vary in size. The influenza ('flu) virus is an example of a large virus. An example of a small virus is the HIV virus.

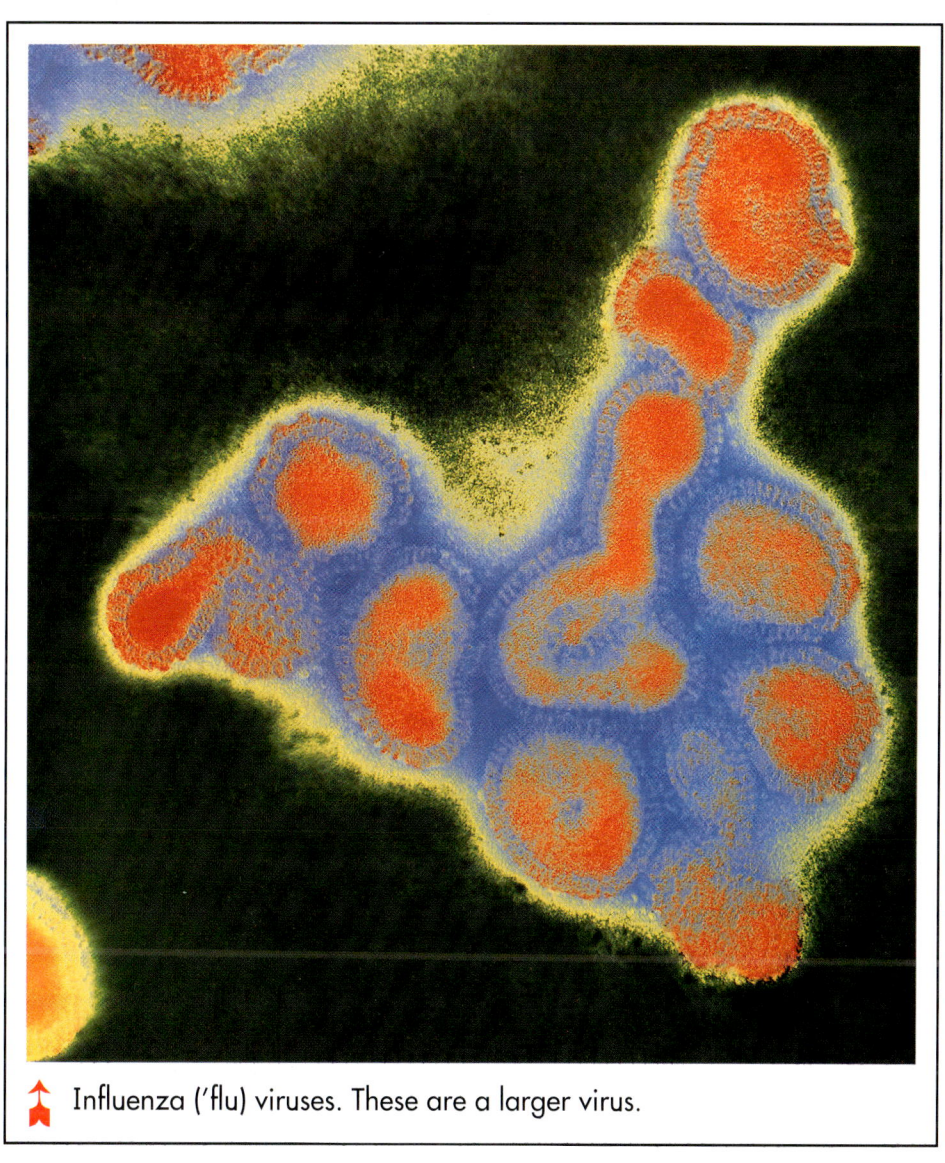

↑ Influenza ('flu) viruses. These are a larger virus.

13 What shape are viruses?

Viruses are not all the same shape. They are not classified by shape like bacteria.

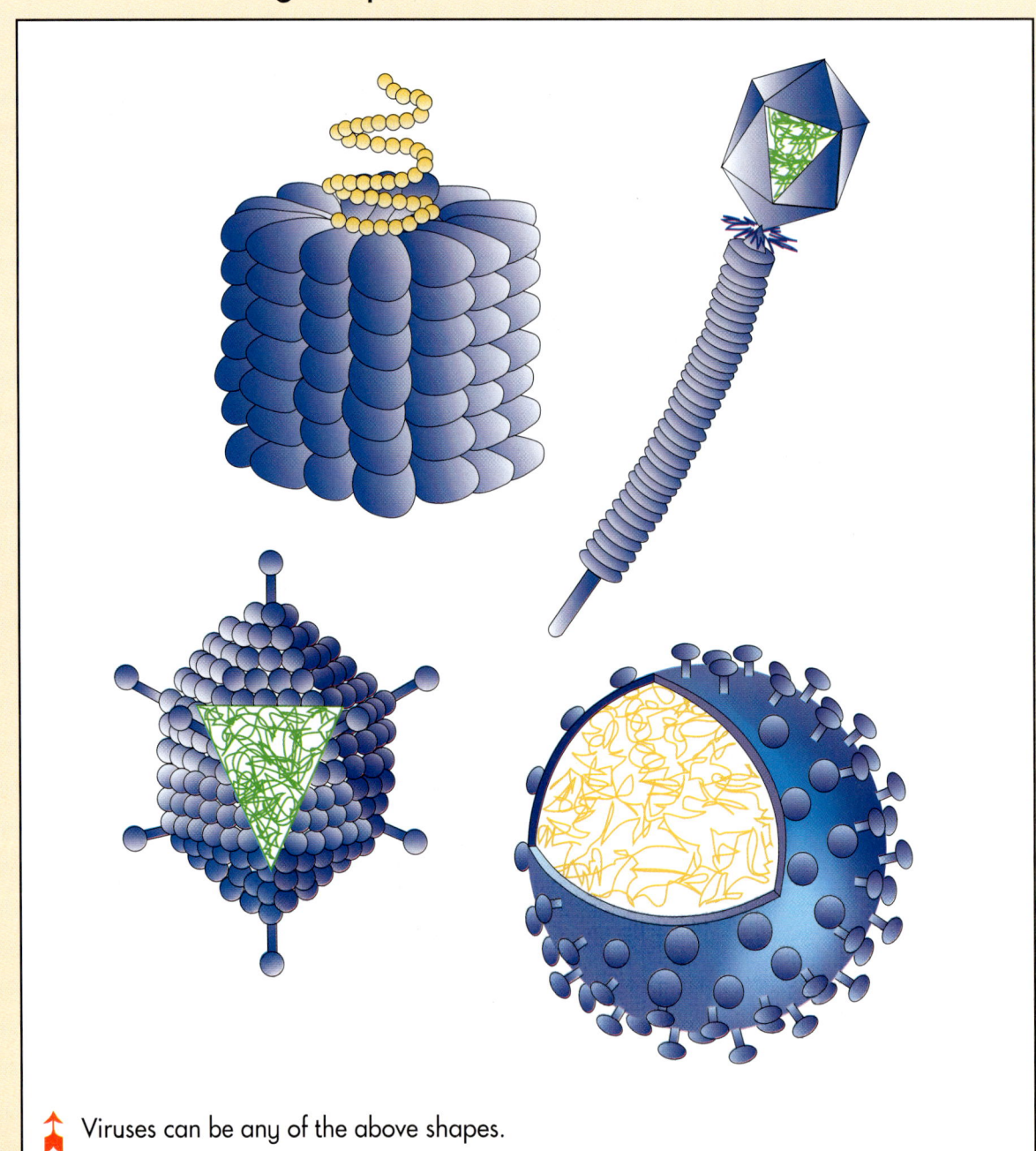

Viruses can be any of the above shapes.

Viruses can be round or they can be long strands. One virus, called a bacteriophage, is shaped like a polyhedron.

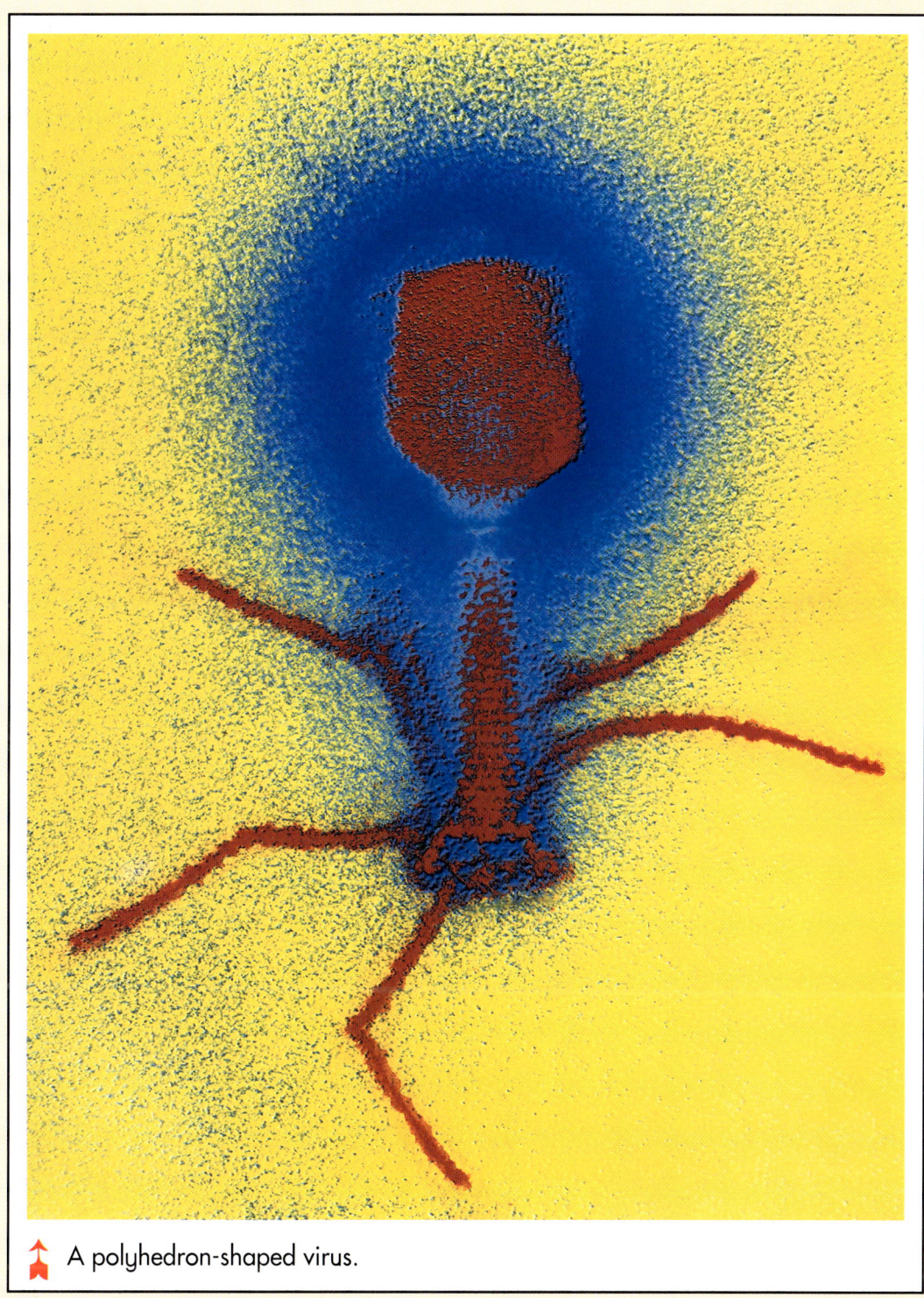

⬆ A polyhedron-shaped virus.

14 Keeping healthy

Regular washing is one important way of keeping ourselves healthy.

Bacteria and viruses are so small that we cannot normally see them. Washing our hands can help prevent them invading our bodies.

Washing

The surface of our skin is covered with harmful bacteria and washing with soap and water cannot remove them all.

Handwashing is a very important way of helping us keep healthy. It is very important to wash our hands after going to the lavatory. This can help prevent bacteria in our stools getting on to our hands.

We must always wash our hands before touching or eating food. This can help stop bacteria getting into our stomachs and making us ill. Bacteria do not like living in a dry environment and so it is important to dry our skin properly.

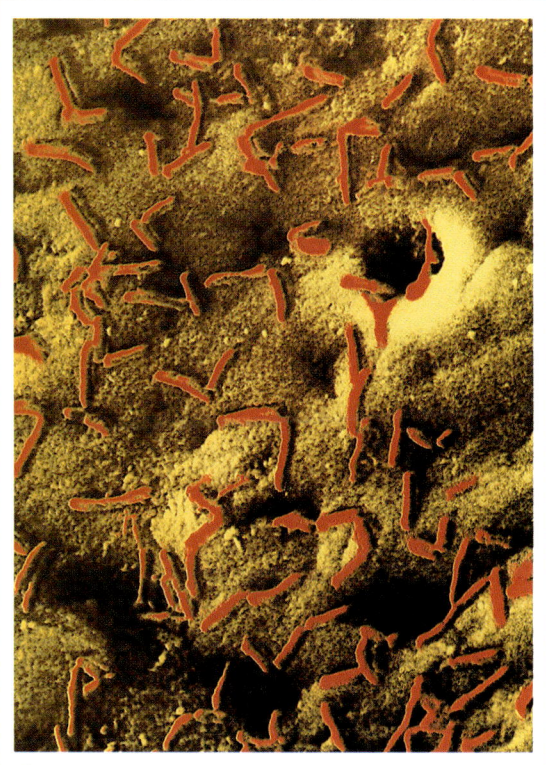

⬆ The red shapes are bacteria on the surface of a human tooth.

If we do not clean our teeth properly, the bacteria in our mouth and throat can produce plaque which sticks to our teeth. This can be very difficult to remove.

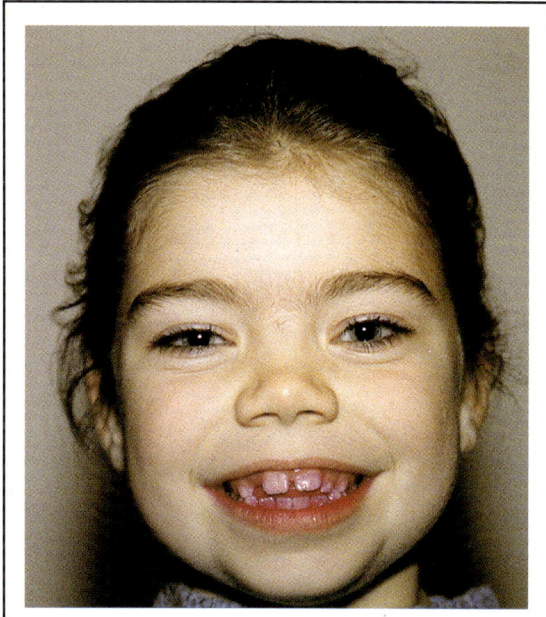

⬆ The pink dye shows up any plaque on the teeth.

Glossary

Antibiotics	An antibiotic is a medicine which destroys bacteria.
Bowel	The bowel is an important part of the digestive system.
Cell	A cell is the smallest unit of any living thing (e.g. a plant or animal).
Colony	A colony is a group of organisms living together.
Digestive system	The digestive system is a set of organs that works together to help us take in food. It then breaks the food down so that we can use it and gets rid of any waste products.
DNA	DNA is a material inside cells. It is necessary for cells to survive.
Drug	A drug is a liquid or powder that is used in medicine to help people get better when they are ill.
Electron microscope	An electron microscope is a very powerful microscope. It allows us to see very small objects which we cannot see using our eyes.
Host	A host is an organism on which a parasite lives.
Immune system	The immune system is the name for the way parts of the body work together to protect us against infection.
Microscope	The microscope is a number of lenses placed in special positions allowing us to see very small objects.
Multiply	To multiply means to reproduce and have young.
Organism	An organism is a living thing.
Parasite	A parasite is a living thing that lives off another living thing.
Phagocyte	A phagocyte is a special type of blood cell which can surround and eat up bacteria.
Plaque	Plaque is a coating of bacteria which can build up on our teeth and can cause gum disease.
RNA	RNA is a material found in cells. Without RNA, cells could not carry out their special roles or jobs.
Stools	Stools are made up of the waste products from our food. They are passed out of our body when we go to the lavatory.
Strand	A strand is a long chain of things joined together to look like a rope.
System	A system is a set of things which work together to perform a particular function.

Toxins — Toxins are chemicals which are poisonous to plants or animals.

Urine — Urine is a liquid made in the kidneys and stored in the bladder until it is passed out of the body when we go to the lavatory.

Vitamins — Vitamins are substances present in food or made by bacteria which help us grow and stay healthy.

White blood cells — White blood cells are a special group of cells which help us fight off harmful organisms or materials which may enter our body.

Further information

Places to visit

Human Biology Exhibition, at
Natural History Museum, London
Open: 10.00 a.m. – 6.00 p.m. (Monday to Saturday)
       11.00 a.m. – 6.00 p.m. (Sunday)

Science for Life, at
Natural History Galleries, Manchester Museum
Open: 10.00 a.m. – 5.00 p.m. (Monday to Saturday only)

Royal Museum of Scotland, Edinburgh

Index

Aa antibiotics 17
antibody 21

Cc colds 19, 20
cuts 14, 22

Dd digestive system 6, 7
diphtheria 12, 13
dysentery 13

Ff fighting bacteria 16
fighting viruses 21
food poisoning 11
'flu 19, 25

Hh harmful bacteria 3, 11, 12, 13, 14, 15, 16, 17
harmful viruses 18, 19
helpful bacteria 3, 4, 5, 6, 7
host 23

Ii ill 20, 21
immune system 15, 16
immunisation 21
influenza ('flu) 19, 25

Mm meningitis 11

Pp phagocyte 16, 17

Rr rod-shaped bacteria 10, 11
round-shaped bacteria 10, 11

Ss salmonella 11, 13
shape 10, 11, 26, 27
size 8, 24, 25
sore throats 11, 19, 20
spiral-shaped bacteria 10, 11

Tt tetanus 12, 13
toxins 15
typhoid 13

Ww washing 28, 29
white blood cells 16